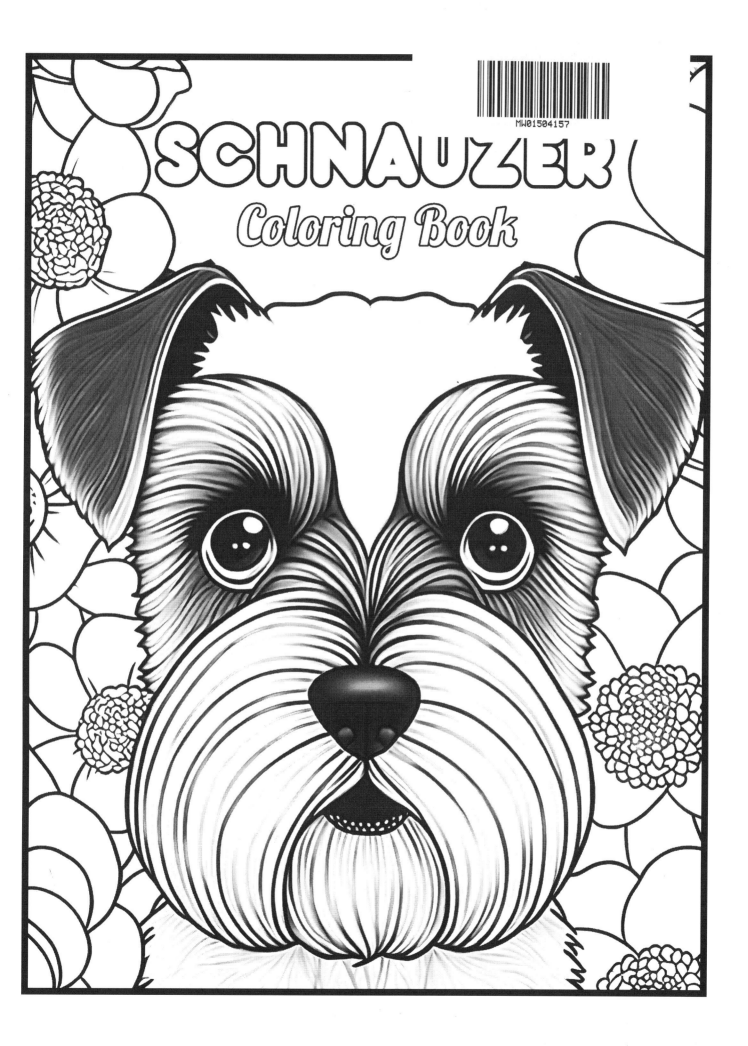

Thank You!

We hope you enjoyed our coloring book!

If so, please take a moment to leave a **REVIEW**.

Your feedback helps us improve!

THANKS FOR YOUR AMAZING SUPPORT!

Scan the QR code below to go directly to our **AMAZON STORE**

Made in United States
Troutdale, OR
03/28/2025